# The Alexandra Sequence

JOHN REDMOND was born and brought up in Dublin. After taking a doctorate in contemporary poetry at the University of Oxford, he spent two years teaching at Macalester College in Minnesota. He was associated for some time with the poetry magazine *Thumbscrew*, and has reviewed poetry for the *LRB*, the *TLS*, the *Irish Times*, and the *Guardian*. He was twice runner-up in the Irish Chess Championship. Currently, he teaches in the English Department at the University of Liverpool.

T0098279

Also by JOHN REDMOND
from Carcanet Press

*MUDe* (2008)
*Thumb's Width* (2001)

# The Alexandra Sequence

JOHN REDMOND

CARCANET

*For Ferdia*

∽

First published in Great Britain in 2016 by
CARCANET PRESS LIMITED
Alliance House, 30 Cross Street
Manchester M2 7AQ
www.carcanet.co.uk

A CIP catalogue record for this book is available from
the British Library, ISBN 9781784102043

The publisher acknowledges financial assistance
from Arts Council England.

Supported using public funding by
ARTS COUNCIL
ENGLAND

# Contents

## The Alexandra Sequence

## Other Poems

# The Alexandra Sequence

# Alexandra
# One

I open a window east of Microsoft Word
—*Room! Room!*—as the father of winter
opens a door—*Give me room to rhyme!*—

and in blow the masks of brotherhood with their
ambivalent question, 'Would you be revived?'
To explicate is to amplify.

—*Welcome fools and goats and quacks,*
*old teapots and chimneystacks!*—Into a… *film?*
(really: some minutes of shaking

shot on a phone) a shadow, call him 'Kris Kringle'
or 'Robin Redbreast' or 'The King of The Waxing Year'
navigates the snugs and nooks

and stamps his cane: *Welcome dames and dolts*
*and mules! Welcome trolls and welcome tools!* The whole
pub blinks *('Did he mean us?')* but nobody bails.

Half with hoods up, half with hoods down,
the regular patrons seem at home—*Ladies*
*and gentlemen, good evening to you all…*—

with masked men bursting in (they've been there).
As the long-cloaked guisers whoop and wheel
(not always widdershins) — *For in comes I,*

*Father Christmas. Ho Ho Ho!* —
grizzled expressions about the jukebox
agree. Now that's their kind of Santa.

They like him all in black.
Who would not admire a Sun King
dressed in sunglasses and a sunhat?

In here, it is three a.m. with nothing on
but my laptop, its lonely chiaroscuro
landing a stretched-out shadow

along angular moons of IKEA.
A refreshing tilt of the screen
carves out of darkness a wrist, a face,

laminates my lack of sleep with the back-lit
pastel icons of Skype and Spotify:
this is togetherness as seen from

the crow's nest. — *And if you don't believe what
I say, in comes St George to clear the way!* —
For a moment, the upload freezes

so the only thing still moving is
a deliquescent blue, a tadpole
chasing its tail. I rise from the screen

and slat back my windows.
The rave in our car park
has been building for hours. A few

stairwells over, the new arrivals
have invited *tout le monde* to
roar at each other. — *Man, this is fucked up!*

*Sick party, man, sick!* — Gold neck-chains,
a girl with Playboy bunny-ears,
over-loud, over-spilling. I suspect

my genteel neighbours spy with me
— *You know me, man, I'm the best
in the world, the whole wide world!* —

as shapes get magnetised ever more
boisterously to one corner or another
of our little no-space. I dial 999

but the voice at the other end is crisp:
'*We are not in the business of shutting
parties down.*' I snap the phone down. Jesus!

I need to remember I'm not in Minnesota
anymore. I need to move, to modify,
(and as for motivation) I need room, room…

Wheeling about a boozer in the near-past,
these pixils offer, if not salvation, then
a renovation of life that is slovenly,

lo-fi. The action (boy kills boy, boy
revives, boy kills boy, girl receives
all the money) has the look of

any true religion: a lobster in a liquidiser
(you might ask: is it turned on?)
St George clouts The Turk — *I'll make mince pies*

*of him!*—The Turk smites St George (to
execute, to vivify) and, when The Doctor
falls in (every movement of the camera

a swirl of murk), Miss Funny, Jack Finney,
and Lucifer boom: *Mince pies hot!*
*Mince pies cold! Send him to the devil*

*when he's nine days old!* Below me,
the inevitable fight erupts; people spin
away to mobile phones, a flow

of bodies across the car park
rippling into a bottleneck opposite.
I ring again—*Can you see any knives?*—

*Not from here, but it looks*
*serious.* —*We're coming!*—A siren
in minutes. After they ring me back

to buzz them in, two policewomen
confront the revellers.—*Take a step back! Step*
*back!*—That will teach them, I think,

and, touching my Blackberry, begin
to film. An athletic twisting shape
elbows the chunkiest cop in the face

so that, in toppling, she stares up
in my direction. Backs slide off
the fronts of cars, a larger van offloads

more law, and shadows flee to the guilty
stairwell. Knock Knock. —*Open the door!*—
The mummery concludes; they pass around

a hat—*All silver and no brass!*—
In the window St George is a-flicker:
*Once I was dead and now I am alive,*

*blessed be The Doctor who helped me revive!*
*We'll all be brothers and fight no more,*
*we'll all shake hands like we did before.*

In a final touch of 'artistry',
the camera tilts so that vertical men
are horizontal. Father Christmas leads a blast

of ''Tis the season to be jolly'. We are family.
We are blurs that would be vivid. We are burrs.
Mummocks in trackies, slackers in NIKE,

shamblers in Celtic tops, twirlies in mufti,
mumchances in baseball caps bearing
the legend of the New York Yankees. Mummers.

# *Alexandra Two*

*Knock knock.* Isn't that how it starts? A hand
tenting the page, a face cheek-boning through?
As father twists inside the caul —

Hallowe'ens ago — to shake his forehead
at the sheeted trick-or-treaters
— *Get away and pray for the souls*

*of the faithfully departed!* — I rise
to ask the other side, *Who's there?*
and, on the stairwell, something stalls

between the on-off green community light
and a god that wears both our faces.
*Sorry to be a pain…* The blonde half of

the new pair on the block goes dark,
goes blonde again, *But do you know*
*where the water-meter is?* Blankly

greeting this gleam of neighbourliness,
I darken back at her. Doesn't she get
what kind of neighbourhood this is?

Nobody round here *knocks.* Down
the judas holes our stairwell sinks
to Toxteth. All the way down — doesn't

she know what that means? *Sorry, no.*
She glows. She vanishes. *Oh right. Ok.*
Goes. Left in a splash of oblivion

I stew on my curmudgeonliness:
Might as well have worn a mask!
Next time, for a more seasonal

impression, leap from the flat,
spines a-bristle from head to foot:
a human porcupine! After all,

the man of straw always makes us
shiver in showing us the arrows
*schwoompf schwoompf* sticking through him.

'There are not enough places in the world
with the word THEATRE written over them.'
Outside in a neighbouring park,

the local hoodies remember their Holub,
exchanging fireworks horizontally,
their Midsummer Night Dreams

merging in mid-air. Yesterday,
as the streetlights came on, I clocked a pair
at the window of a dorm (knock knock)

pushing the caul back with their hands,
their grips evolving towards iPads,
iPhones... until something spooked them

and they broke away with nothing.
I approached the junction at right-angles;
they walked at right-angles towards me,

when (it was too quick not to be chance)
a lone police car swung onto our road.
The boys suddenly came over all casual,

(method acting) depressing with elaborate
ceremony the button at the crossing —
*After you* — the car, accordingly, gearing down

to purr: *No, no, after you.* So I ran
across and rapped on the glass — *Those kids
just tried to break in over there!* — Down my

jittery reflection a professional mien
rolled — *Ok, thanks!* — and accelerated away
even as our friends were already sprinting

across the park. How to live here?
The stairwell echoes all the way down.
Behind the caul the community light

comes on, comes off, the two shapes
of yesterday appearing, disappearing against it.
They bring back to me another morning

finicky with wind chimes and ramekins;
little dips and water biscuits; carrot-strips,
tsatsiki. On Stephen's Day we expected

visitors. Influx of freckled hands. A pair
of blackened faces over Adidas trainers.
Glinting avarice. Speckles of a Sun King

in a sparsely ribboned jar: *The Wren, the Wren,*
*the King of All Birds, on Stephen's Day*
*is caught in the furze, though he is little*

*his spirit is great, so rise up mister and* ... still
not knowing where the water-meter is
I protrude through the caul of my father

to give the nothingness ten pence (each).

# Alexandra
# Three

The sound of Pavement begins on the sun
with the music of chainsaws over the Resurrected One.
In its easy confusion of seasons, the so-called

'Winter Version' of 'Summer Babe' survives
the residual fuzz of its own demise,
falling backwards into a new skin, as I nudge

the car into the way of exploding blocks
of water, bright slabs of cleanliness flung
by the attendant. Ten minutes here, and that's

me. Lovely to muse, though, for a spell,
with the windscreen evolving and dissolving
in slovenly ovals, the sun sliding through

the Bridget Riley patterns of suddy liquid
to write me out in waves of zebra-shadow.
Not all music survives a move. While this

or that 'real me' snares in the cat-flap stringily,
whole periods of listening crumble in the removal van.
How miserable to grant once-sacred atmospheres

a last chance—anxiously loading track after track
until—there!—we re-live the first feeling
of having known it always. It is a reliving,

always, to hear what we never heard
through what we no longer hear. So, however early
in Pavement's career, we take the song's

hint that we were has-beens all along... that
'start with the farewell tour and take it from there'
vibe. 'Very dirty car', the cheeky ragamuffin

hose-bearer opines. Defensively I gesture
to bits and pieces of the new me, the splashes
of ghostly experience strewn across the roof

objecting, 'I have to park under trees', and adding,
in the face of his leering scepticism, '*Lime* trees'.
As he turns the water-cannon on me,

(full-force—with ill-disguised glee) I am
blasted backwards into the street (at least
psychologically) and the last twenty years

since I swayed to the governors of lo-fi
with my once-best pal, 'The Lord of the Flies'
(competitive friendships of young men,

how they fly apart, run down in patches of crud,
seldom revive). Out of the saturated colours
of 'Carrot Rope', the Pavement guys strolled

towards us wearing their bright yellow
oilskins as though to say, The world,
even in direct sunlight, is not worth tautening

over. When he crawled across the roof
with a playful smile I used to find Mark Ibold
the most simpatico, though I liked too the gestures

of Stephen Malkmus as he struck the imaginary ball
out of the imaginary park. It was clear who was
Father Winter here. Even so, in the play

of loose equations maybe we confused
laziness for angelic lassitude... what did
it say about us that we didn't want

*them* to succeed too much, too openly?
Was it selfish to hail their self-sabotage
(to hug it to ourselves, even) knowing

that the punchline (you don't *know*
how many Indie musicians it takes
to change a light-bulb?) picked us off?

From that first time I saw Malkmus
sing angstily side-on — band and audience
in the corner of either eye, suspecting

that not exactly everyone could be
the Resurrection — to last year in Brixton
was quite the sea-change — such was the

luminous mood of middle-aged wellbeing
our hero had even rotated a little. Over the
upraised hands, outsize beachballs

slopped about in slo-mo, and Jane,
rising to smack one from below, fell
backwards into a well of others, into

their songs of ourselves, their offers
of an everlasting amplitude. Have we, then,
found our level? Where the trees make their slow

sandwich (roots bursting sidewalk, trunks
cracking side-walls) my preternaturally
shiny car delivers us down the shadiest

of lanes (Linnet, Lodge, Lark) for our first
time in The Moon and Pea. Queuing
on the street we wonder, who will we be?

What to make of the shaved heads and dungarees,
the pastel chairs (non-identical), the
super-bright air of an adult play-room?

Enhancements of life (hey, check out the
granola) spill into what we are just as,
each morning, the seeds fly the windscreen

and once more from the lot my 'poet's car'
is last to leave. Whether living or
surviving, we will take the serendipity every time:

that my wife-to-be hails from Newcastle-
Under-Lyme and likes nothing better than
the heat of a dark Honda Civic against a south-facing wall.

# *Alexandra Four*

Other than skew-whiff lanterns floating by
with answers—at different elevations—
to the question, 'What will we make

next year?' most of the night-sky—the
conflagrations shaped like crabs and spiders,
the tempestuous wisps and sweeps, all

those glittering chunks, whipped up, swirled about—
happened long ago and (tell us slowly—
you know we are slow) is stretching

away from us at an ever-faster rate.
*Exactly* how old we are—that, too, is lost
in the doughy stretching of hot and cold,

though, as our losses show: to keep
pace with things is something in this universe,
and the only explosion we have to believe in—

the first expression of where and when—
weaves in our faces at every moment, every
unlikely twist of the head; everything

wound through with it: the cameraphone—
years out of date—in your right hand;
the five-year-old hand in your other—

all livid with accident; every stillness
crawling with collisions, speeds crawling
over and under speeds, under moods

to the invisible grinding of other gears.
Out of the blue dark, bodies pour
and pick with us across the muck;

not finding a way, just flowing, half-
forward, half-backward, passing through
each other's directions so that the friends

we see every other year, caught up
in the scrummage, lend us, at awkward
stages, their dog, their children.

'Sam, keep your light-sabre on!' Though he
swings it about insanely, lighting up
the arms of strangers, and leaps out hissing

in front of his sister's pram—sacred
custom by now—the vivid play
of blue-red gulps helps navigate

an October evening with no centre,
where everything seen drifts to one side.
Even the Palm House with its freakish

arboreal exotica, a great spaceship
of nineteenth-century glass
stretched apart with where and when,

slides quickly from a corner of the eye,
as the zombie drummers grandly come,
thumping zombie-slow — *boom chaka boom* —

implausible mongers of doom — summoned
(with a good chunk of the city) via slumps
and shoulders of Victorian landscaping

to the Festival of Lights, this one day
of the year when, as the flyer has it,
'the door to the dream-world is left open'.

In one chiaroscuro scene after another,
families bear aloft as paper lamps
the homemade fantasies of childhood:

a half-fish; a scooped-out skeleton;
the sloppy baguettes of a softening star —
so the friends we somehow managed

halfway through our lives can read
where we are at, can slow down
(with the bony light shaking

from a Neolithic horse), can match
our speed in the hard-to-credit: the
half-accident of a house by the park.

Where we walk is where we walked
hours ago in daylight, when Bertie
sprinted off to goad the slower dogs —

'Maybe *we* should have a whippet…' —
with the moment we first met —
'Nyah must have slept through it all' —

still travelling from its centre —
'Well, I vote labrador' — and consigned
to minor developments around the eyes —

'Come down to see us, come down next
time' — And, when we next meet up,
who will be more or less behind...?

On the far side of the lake, illuminated
by little skiffs of fire, we wait
for ourselves, or whatever we choose

to make of ourselves, to materialise,
and I secure my grip on the lurcher,
as he divines a half-chewed burger

or something else slung from the occasion
and all of the beings which bind him
together try to heave away.

# Alexandra Five

'I prefer the way they do things in Tibet' —
he says (although he doesn't), and we
don't (but we say it). After chess

 has done with speaking through us, when we
 sprawl in the pub downstairs, out
of gas, with the shadows of tumbleweed

 rolling extravagantly over us, our faces
 alive with execution, admiring the intentions
we have carved into each other,

 between the swells of non-conversation
 to which we are well-accustomed —
'Tricky, isn't it?' 'It is difficult, yes.' —

 the creator is apt to slide (Mondays, The
 Caledonia, from seven) his silence-filling
silence-filler-killer. Which

 he might have been about to try (and didn't)
 that Monday when the chess club
scattered to the cry — 'It's kicking

off on Smithdown!'—and, scrambling
out for taxis, met with a surprise
all on one side: the police cars

sliding into 'Vs' their magic roundabouts
of blue (as they slid thirty years before)
to prevent all travel to 'the front'—our

sketchy haircuts and silhouettes flying through
what we could while we could—out-of-focus,
no direction—fragmenting down the rabbit hole

of Prince's Road by gardens already
manned and vibrant; the next-doors outside
getting high on midnight hits of

solidarity; all in the minutes before
the frail arcs of petrol bombs, the shaken-
down shop-chainmail, the drivers

yanked from unlit cars brought home to them
(from further away than ever) the rioters
I wanted to see and wouldn't—even

on Youtube where their jittery light
and sound gave way to *Britain's
burning!* on national television. With

nowhere to go but their own
no-go neighbourhood the young men
circled inside what I had circled

around when I moved to Alexandra
(turning one street corner away
into three). '1982 all over again,'

the taxi-driver told me days later.
'That police-station?' 'Yeh?' I said.
'Tried to torch it. Mind you, *proper*

hardcore—there were… I dunno…
*twenty*. The rest were followers.'
I nodded back. 'It's tricky, isn't it?'

Before driving to Ireland I enter
a (mildly toasted) supermarket
to buy a house for my niece (she

turns three). On its sky-blue side
'Shop' is written in large red letters
and there are luminous emblems

of ice cream and candy. Within seconds
it is a mad success: her little
sisterhood—falling, sitting—agrees

to outlaw boys then, swimming as
a pack behind the plastic walls,
topples them—end over end—

about my brother's new kitchen
where the hirsute arms of the gods descend
for an occasional stretch of decorum.

Gradually circumnavigated,
the only small boy in the room
rotates his head to watch them go

and, as we come face to face,
his expression is saying, 'it's tricky',
and mine is lost in Tibet.

# Alexandra
# Six

'I am dead at present...,' my father remembers to say,
walking through me, with the end of a tail
in his one good hand— '...and he will be

dead, dead-ed, dead-ed-ed...'—pause,
look down, permit the distinction to
deepen his voice—'...presently.' Small,

I wondered how it would feel to be
swung by a bendy part of myself
up and away from an outhouse wall—

swoosh of sky, of sea—then, more briskly,
down and towards, as the transparency
of my father—of his whole design—

repeatedly smashed the mouse's head.
Under the basement ceiling, where I
lay projecting these bits and pieces

on the life rarely seen (but endlessly
heard) in the floorboards above, I'd
spy amidst the cameos and do-overs,

the flashes back and forward, this one
our trap deflected more than forty
years ago, with all his fragments

still bothering to struggle even as
the living mice materialised, passed by.
When their colony first mushroomed — stop

the lights! We were surrounded, infested.
I no longer stayed up late in case
one leapt out, 'jus' like tha'!' (à la

Tommy Cooper). Where they went the walls
would crackle from within. I could feel
the hairs on my body react with an inkling.

Months after we slaughtered them all
I'd stop and listen for what kept me
listening months before: a tell-tale

step, a slither, like the intelligence
of raindrops on a pane, which could
sniff the silence up and down to find

the slightest chink. Even as he kept
the blue goo flooding shoe-sized
white containers (all that remained

when we moved out), Mal, our rented
killer, kept the black jokes flowing
beneath his drill-sergeant moustache.

He would crumple his face and squeak, 'We
wuz here first!' and then in his own voice:
'I have been here before, you know...' (pause

to add bass) '…doing 'big fellas'.'
But that was in another life.
When things were at their pre-Mal

stickiest I remember how we poured,
over specially-bought gum-paper,
a slick of sugar and cocoa to skulk,

come lights out, on the kitchen floor.
That night the weird banshee cry
of a creature in trouble forced

us awake to taste the damage.
The mouse itself looked freshly made —
its gawpy mouth opening and closing,

tiny fists flexing like mad, unable
to move. Misery. And it fell to us
to put him out of it. I cast

around for something weapon-like
and, with Jane shouting from the side,
loomed over the floor in a gothic tableau:

The Executioner Raises his Broom.
Freakiest then to hear the rest of them —
a hitherto unknown little army —

making of the wall an ersatz beehive.
Swatting down, I stuck fast (sod's law),
lifted up the suppurating crust

as one great mass (sword-in-stone-style)
then, panicking, crashed it down
jus' like tha', jus' like tha' — Jane

shaking now, my wet T-shirt holding on,
all desperate to quit this cul-de-sac —
until nothing could survive the swinge

of the broom and the much-buffeted
bin shook to an agricultural dump.
When it was done we stood a while,

staring down at the bodies we sometimes
mistake as our own. — 'Didn't have
time to tidy him up.' — With a brief

turn as his own mortuary attendant
my ever-versatile father flickers
above me on the floorboards — 'I have

dead-ed him …' — before getting back
into character (his own) with a few
slices of family grammar — '… so he

has been dead-ed-ed'. Slumping down
gingerly on the see-through trolley, really
digging deep, he lets his mouth fall open

and adopts an expression of having to
do something he wouldn't normally dream
of doing—his one good paw hanging down

from the side — empty as I remember.

# Alexandra
# Seven

The lemon's nostalgia for the poppy-seed
is a memory of the placenta. The grapefruit
fills, as the grape foretold, with the incandescence

of not going back—the hemispheres light up,
veined with epigrams, as though needing to
get it over, although there is no getting over

the see-through golden age—the seasons of
the fig and lentil fold inwards, self-enclose—
the mountain range shadows come and go

across the surface of the melon
as slow and over-the-top as an everlasting pastoral.
A warehouse close to the airport

seems wrong—'Put your hand there—
feel that?'—We park like plane-spotters
in the chain-linked sun—'He's stopped

moving… no, hang on, he's doing
something!'—and stay in the car as long
as we can. Upstairs in a circle, eight

women and eight men — 'Hi! I'm Dan,
I teach.' 'Zora here — I'm a doctor.' —
invent the day-glo laminate of

your first day. While some of the ladies
rock up and down on giant balls,
our instructor kneels across the highs and lows

of labour… we are going back (at last)
to being the right size, passing from hand
to hand a doll (easy to twist

and turn) that takes on all the faces
in the room. 'Thinking of a home birth?
Put up your hand!' — nobody moves, but

part of Jane leaps a centimetre.
Once you were between names, a seahorse
half-translated into an ashen negligee

and, stickily prescient, insinuated
into twilight the evanescent shovel of
our coming-together, by beginning

to separate your fingers. Now you have a whole
portfolio of movement; with my no-longer
transparent hand I tap the dome two

or three times and you walk me through
my privilege with a tremor, admit me to
your confidences with a pantheon of up

and down gulps, suave gravities, strategic
slumps, by which you have come to judge:
the other side of skin is everything.

We had been in the house six months.
The rose-bushes the old couple had left to us
had been and gone; the gypsophila had come

and gone; the sky-blue phlox taken down
from their burst trellis; the greenhouse dishevelled
with jasmine we malleted out of this world;

the aggravated blues of two police-cars
about to come and go — brief December blooming —
the winter-flowering cherry blossom ready

for its deliverance; myself keeping warm,
by reading with the blinds down, shivering
into the Twelfth Satire, where Juvenal,

to celebrate his friend's reprieve from
shipwreck, invokes the altar of turf on which
he will sacrifice two lambs, a calf fresh

from its mother, and — had he the cash —
an ox so grotesquely fat only some
musclebound priest could slice its neck when

there was a crash — not in the original but
outside. I flipped up the screen and there he stood —
looking at me with eyes he didn't always have;

the knife in his no-longer webbed hand
gouging the frame; a single-glazed vision
of otherness so fast my sense of his

junkie paleness was of a turning-aside,
a blur of bog-standard trackies and beanie
vaulting the rose-festooned wall,

as I ran backwards into the still-
ungutted kitchen shouting, 'Get out
of here mate!' feeling with one hand

for the police, the other for a carving-knife
sticky with mango. Evolution, no? Where
the village woodcarvings come bending

through the mist, you can tell the winning parts of
losers because they start to drip. It is rare to get
the first time right: the pteranodon's beak

crashes down in a jungle of third and fourth goes;
the greengage take a running leap across
the foam-mouthed roar of pumpkins

and, in his expulsion of the rebel angels,
Brueghel has arranged the winged crowds
tumbling end over end through the dawnlight

to include blowfish and upside-down squid,
puzzled armadillos facing backwards
greyhounds shrivelling to frogspawn,

saints and sinners reborn as sesame seeds.
Wandering past the windows of The Blob
Shop, I try to see the old guys – burping

like turtles in the middle of the day—
always there!—with the clemency
of your mother's eyes (whether you

have them or not) then swing by the market
through the rows of satsumas, step
over ripped-open boxes of nectarines

and yams, to a new way of being
on my own. How else should we start
in on the long-ago—and then the not-so—

but over a suggestion of gypsophila?
A convolution of greenness, a room
with enormous windows at either end

looking through itself—where we stood
with the old couple reminding us of
themselves: Arnie and his sofa renewing

their vows ('Can't see us moving!') while Pat
slowly shook her head: 'Never mind him, love,
he can't even get up them stairs.'

Halfway up the same, Jane, beginning
to falter, makes her three wishes—'I
just want to bend over, tie my shoelaces

and have a glass of wine!'—at which you
undulate subtly, keeping schtum:
anyone's idea of your father's son.

From the maverick sorrow of being
one inch long to the rejuvenations
of Rome under the Antonines, even such

an august word as 'solvency' is at more
than one remove from the scented altitude
of the orangerie—like those mosaic floors

(so mesmeric on *Time Team*) plotting
the achievements of the plough in the smashed
tessera of their enterprise. To open doors for you

a splash of white powder remains where we
laid waste a wasps' nest. We re-conceive
the windows from scratch (no

more wood!), gut the kitchen. Walk around
as dust-ghosts, get under the house's
papery skin. Re-wire. Likely re-bid

(against its owner) for a baby-changer
on eBay. Consign the bijoux civilisation
of the Moses Basket (*not* for transporting

you downstairs) to the plans of an ancient
porousness that already bears you in mind.
And still I think of him, still running

away—the police dogs breathing salvation—
the former lentil hunted down by former
poppy-seeds, a fugitive beyond the delphinium,

our hypericum unravelling in bee-smoke, the
blossoming phlox and gypsophila, the goldenrod
and Nellie Moser, things the old couple didn't know

had been grown to find you in—fragments
of your saga now with this ménage of
household deities: an artificial hedgehog,

a bluish overturned tortoise (just so),
and—on the side of the shed forever
in shade—a burnt-out sun god hanging

on his plate. Fat-faced, like some eighteenth-
century despot, he wears a rusty nail
through his forehead—his compline

a stray reflection when the glass door
slides open — his vespers a pollinated spell
burrowing through the perfumes and flavours

that wait for you, Ferdia, in the aubretia.

# Other Poems

# The Big Freeze

Quirky how
you want to hear my horse-laugh.
Distantly, we download
a space-photograph
of Britannia
frozen to her broomstick.
At either end of it
we're stuck.

The level of falling is set to continue.
'When *did* Scooby Doo
enter our relationship?'
From a window below
'our' dopeheads bestow
yellow-dark gobs
on the slush.
'Was it after Sebadoh?'

'You got them on in the background?'
'Hey, we're slackers (cough)… I suppose.'
'No. We're slobs.'
Spotified lo-fi
fizzles down the aromatic stairwell.
'Chicken, do you want me to become a Catholic?'
Into my slovenly Nokia I neigh.

# Once a Cloud

Once a cloud
love happens now.
How we evolved
Colosseums ago
is a question
these altocirrus
models of our
every move
impose, my dear,

blowing overhead.
The evening sky's
a feast of making
where we make out
our unicorn selves,
colossal and slow,
developing holes
like a Henry Moore.

Down here too
where foreplay
is lit by afterglow
the clouds I give you
have nowhere to go,
expanding a future
of indigo shadow:
a softer St Peter's.

# Avatar

'What must be strange?'
Under the dragon wings
and raptor-beaks
of Her Majesty's still-surviving fleet—
'To talk about yourself
in the plural'—we bob
and sway
with all the kids, the couples.
'The third person, even.'

England's only island-city:
from the other side of the universe
an armoured vest waves down at us
and the many anchors outweigh
our vegetarian cafe.
Enough red meat: it is
'almost time for the matinee.'
Beneath the dragon wings of

*Apocalypse Now*
and raptor-beaks
of *Blade Runner*, the cinema
is aswarm
with glasses over glasses.
A kiss, during
the slushier bits of *Avatar*,
is a hybrid form
of shield-play:
I shut one eye—now you—
as a god might use the royal 'we'.

# Kieran's Day

As a saint is remembered
    by holes in the cloud-shadow

shouldering down the hill
    for fifteen hundred years

to brighten—one after the other—
    graveyard, pub, harbour,

you enter the world of shapes
    (today it is our village), boy

we met six weeks ago, so
    endlessly pleased by your hands

you lift them to your face
    and turn them over. Things refresh…

great to see it so busy, to have
    such trouble parking; forms of

sunlight, dust, and saltwater,
    walk out in front of the car;

your mother's phone in her
    mother's hand snaps another

just to be sure; your (living)
    grandfather in his jittery

cricket hat invents new ways
    to wheel you through the throng,

while your other (Irish)
   grandfather, leaning backwards,

extracts a shadow from his mouth
   and puffs out. A slow expansion

between hill and harbour,
   the pub plays host to those

springing up and sitting down
   who need but eye the water to know

the wind's too strong—ah, it is—
   but they could be racing soon.

Dimly hoping to be recognised,
   I push down past enormous

sea-facing windows to the
   business end and signal a half.

When the pressure of the scrum
   makes me snatch whatever comes,

an old man, wheeling on his
   barstool, asks, 'Is that your pint?'

On a day like this we all have form.
   With half his face engulfed

by bug-like sunglasses, our
   neighbour peers into your pram

and affirms (with a brisk nod
   to the graveyard) that he has 'been

above,' and walked seven times about
    Kieran's Cross, 'saying a prayer

or thinking about things or what
    have you…,' but unable

to make out his eyes neither
    you nor I can settle into

the conversation — so we opt
    for all-purpose affirmative

smiles. There was a post office.
    That's gone. An inn. A petrol pump.

Gone. Two pubs. One now. And this
    morning, in the last shop of three,

they let me imitate my father
    ordering Sweet Afton in Irish.

'Been fierce hard,' the owner said,
    'the last few years. Fierce hard.'

We could stay in the pub — watch
    from there — but, with the feeling

of walking into an aftermath,
    aim your pram into the blow.

Clambering out across parked boats,
    purposeful men make their way,

then climb back beaming loudly —
    a muscularity in which we try

to read prequel from sequel.
    As I brake the pram side-on

the apologetic parp of a horn
    seems to ask: 'Is this the beginning?'

Given another six weeks, you
    will be able for a pattern in

time as well as one in space —
    your mother's hair on the pier

going everywhere, your grandmother
    behind a fresh explosion

of plaits, but today (being an event)
    has come too early for you

and hundreds of years too late.
    As though launched from underwater,

a currach materialises at last
    with three men aboard. Roughly

twentysomething, they wear a slew
    of provisional colours (no day-glo,

no lycra, no purpose-built
    gloves). Presently, the tar

hides and ultra-pale oars
    of four currachs herd together

and, in a fever of warming up,
    dash out against the wind

then allow it to blow them back
    vaguely towards the harbour.

On one boat, so much at right-
    angles to us it seems missing

a dimension, two men in oilskins
    gesture side by side to start

the race. But the weather rebuffs
    the currachs straightaway — they go

skew-whiff and, softly crashing
    together, men look left and right

though a rickety wigwam of oars.
    Again they try. Again. When only

one boat is baulked, that's good
    enough! Now there is no turning

back as they beat their way out
    towards a lurid speck which marks

halfway. They are followed
    by the referee's boat which hangs

out to one side, and two or three
    vessels ready in case of accidents.

Sufficiently fanned out, the racers
    point in different directions —

it is anybody's guess which
    has the lead. Expertly timing

their arrival from the pub, a crowd
    mushrooms... the feathered sausage

of a microphone is borne aloft...
    to indicate we are not on TV

but at least we are on the radio.
    Later, your English grandfather,

having hung back for the prize-
    giving, will conclude his inspection

of local sportsmanship and face:
    'So what were you expecting?

'Hip hip hooray!? Three cheers for
    the bravos!?' And, alternately smiling

and sipping his drink, will reply,
    'It was very revealing in many ways.'

In the run for home the crews
    strive for an imaginary line between

an orange buoy and where we
    sway on the pierhead. Close in terms

of the race, the two leaders are
    widely separated in terms of water.

Gruff cheers. 'Good man, Josie!'
    'Yes, Donal, *that's* it. *That's* it!!'

Every stroke has a meaning—
    hugging hands to their chins

then shoving away, the men lean back so far—
    almost to the horizontal—

as though they could leave the world
    of shapes. One boat, the further off,

crosses the 'line', but its victory
    is not clear until the nearer

crew, scarcely a second behind,
    alters their body language. An oarsman

snaps his head back, forward—swearing—
    and the losers crash casually almost carelessly into

the harbour wall, listlessly and reluctantly
    detaching themselves from under your pram

what does it matter now... from under the tonnes of stone...

# Woodworm Inferno

There is a fine, our neighbour advised,
for opening a door to the sun.
The spring tide overtakes this one,
bearing off across the grass
the lengthening splinters of inwardness.

The stumps we make of well-made things...

I like the way you want to burn
back to how things must have been,
the original angle
of every barnacle...

Another dresser, another chair
appears to fall asleep
and vanish.

Tonight on varnished deal
in a newly tiled
and vacuumed room,
we will sit and wait
till our neighbour arrives —
our faces masked with soot.

Listen to the symphony of holes.

# Bouillon

Your childhood all comes back to me
in the shadow of the castle: slow passageways
into the blue, the winter slides, the open
secrets at closing time, the car tyre crammed
with cousins thundering downhill
to crash against home in triumph.
With Ardennes forest
                    lifting on all sides,
we meet the poet over free champagne.
A happy skull from the nursing home,
in boater and purple silk tie,
he launches his first book at ninety-six.
'Of the dandy tradition', you confide.
The town, as every year, is besieged
by the Middle Ages. Dressed as Crusaders,
the grown-up cousins offer to refill
and we consent to suffer 'death by hospitality'.
At night we sit out by the bridge—*this one*
*drinks too much, that one sleeps around*—
and watch the local police, with their pink
day-glo truncheons, serenely misdirect
the traffic.
           Along the firework-reflecting river
the visitors go toe-to-toe, willing the castle
to be stormed by light and sound. We flee
to the non-tourist quarter (head-high
weeds of the old railway station) and halt at a dive.
The wafery landlord, ex-legionnaire, empties
his mind in place of a greeting. Here, paint-pots
and plywood seem to say: if you want
to fit in, act like you don't want to.
And we don't want not to.
                Tied to the front door

and bored with chasing his tail,
a little dog on a retractable leash
draws crazy tripwires across the floor
so the locals must keep looking down
if they want to live.

# The Staircase

Let us take the staircase down into the blue, abysmal sky of Paul Celan
as the contents of this town come loose, come alive

without gravity. Let us idle down a spiral like the DNA of time,
on rungs that are wrought-iron and see-through, in clothes of less

than usual use—your T-shirt (is that too much?), my ski-
jacket (too little?) Let us settle to a depth where the clouds go

upside-down, and the mad glow of home is blocked out
by the tumble of tropical fish, to-do lists, and grossly

uprooted cathedrals. Let us find ourselves—at last—
where we find ourselves alone, in synch with the gestures

of ski-jackets and T-shirts as they complete ever wider turns
in nothingness like guests at some party that has radically

over-spilled. Let us take the staircase down till the stars
close in and the sun drifts further away. Let us feel our

descent to the final rung—here, take my hand—and walk
into it again: outlined hedges; a distant car alarm;

a traffic-light surging to orange. Stairs have their dark side,
like anything else,
                    but that's not the end of the world.

# The Lodge

I surface in the toilet
of the toy house where I lived
and watch myself spray down
the porcelain-sided years.
'Hullo… anyone home?'
How often I would race
*(shit)* 'Just a minute!' *(drip)*
in frosted windowlight
*(finish, finish, just…)*
to fiddle up my zip.

A fist-sized sink, a roll
of paper half played-out
on the floor. As ever,
the whole is audible
inside *and* out, the queer
acoustics of the space, so
near to the front door
(and even the front gate),
that a visitor's well-knit mask
of genteel courtesy risked
a gross, explosive flush,
a porter's grim emergence:
'St Anne's?' 'No. St Hugh's.'
'Ah. Might it be possible

to stroll through the gardens?'
'It might.' For this toy house
was my house (weekends,
three till ten), this crack through
which world and college
dribbled on each other.
Customers did not tip

although, *once*, a taxi driver,
who shuffled in, short-taken,
paid to use the toilet
my mind is in again, where
the rest of me might be —
still fiddling (you can hear this).

# The Night Porter

'...ancient Janus, with his double face
And bunch of keys, the porter of the place.'

—Dryden, *Aeneid*

As he hit the step my head would spin
so that my angrier face met his, so that
my easier face could live, Janus-like,
in the compound glow of video-screens.
Looking up from numbered drawers,
the keys pretended not to see. Each
would hug its copy close as I exhumed
the master-bunch, and flung it down—
all eyes and teeth mixed up—both my
faces grinning at his 'Fuck off, Irish git.'

Against stocking-heads and balaclavas
our security cameras trolled over buddleia
and pergola, though all we ever knew
were blemishes of black and grey—inscrutable
as those the experts probe for origins
of life, the sunless bumps of abyss-walls
taken by the upside-down robot-vehicle.

# Rogue Lock

Such a door
to rebuff me —with a hint
in its knots
of obversity.
Towards my glittering bunch
tremendous oblong
shadows
sprang from the wood.
The lock was rogue.
Master after master

froze. Frustration
rang for corridors
as I blundered towards
the final key: one
with a sleepy-eyed
and solemn look
like me.
I pushed him in.
Scratches rose
on my skin.
As the whole bunch

roared encouragement,
and rich, outrageous
college-shadows
churned the grain,
I tested it,
and twisted it.
But such a door!
It snapped my proxy off
and swallowed him.

When I knelt my eye
to the eye of the obstacle,
my little self
could not be seen. But
in the bloodied
keyhole tunnel,
a tiny door

shut.

# *Avril*

Her staircase. Off a dog-leg corridor.

'Come in, little ones, come in!'

So thrilled by your arrival. By anyone's. Hands in the air, waving crazily—a cartoon witch casting an experimental spell. The small boy's head, on her small boy's body, bobbing Woody Allen glasses about.

Welcome to 'The Shop'. A poetry workshop (minus the 'work').

Your first move always the same: a brief squeeze of greeting, a glance at those present, then straight to the back room for 'supplies': a cardboard box full of *Hula-hoops*, crisps, *Rancheros*; six-packs of beer with harder stuff to one side. Wine her choice, though—and often yours.

Usually yours.

Her part of the ritual to enter slyly, to ply you (first) with the requisite corkscrew (then) with serpentine questions. Gossip about participants absent (and, sometimes, not so *sotto voce,* present). Her stature, close-in, always a surprise. Her way of looking up at you with tilted head, deploying a theatrical, basset-hound seriousness which never lasted long—'Oh yessss, I kept telling him... but what can you dooooo?' In semi-private moments, her voice (capable of a stepped-on-cat's squawk) entering a comic, lower register worthy of Kenneth Williams—'Don't I knowwww it?'

Older than she acted.

Younger than she looked.

A return to the bright front room. On one side, plate-glass portals; on the other, high 1960s 'letterbox' windows. Hardly in the style of her beloved Renaissance Italy but the room's modernist feel a reinforcement of the Shop's 'extra-to-Oxford' effect. Otherwise, donnish normality. Sloping books. Standing-lamps. An impossible family of chairs. And a slippy rug forcing intricate, shifting movements out of us, when going for more beer. As though none of us ever quite stable.

A refuge for you, a refuge for others, in those early Oxford days. You with the little platoon of regulars. You with the drifting army of occasionals. Bar Avril (and one aging hippie) everyone a student. Your poems, their poems, about cod and synaesthesia, about ghosts and Africa and home. Or else not poems at all—bits of novel, of short-story, extracts from a civil-servant's journal salvaged (some wet afternoon) from an antique shop. Your voices, theirs. The hippie blasting out his fifteen-minute chant: 'Hu-*man*! Hu-*man*! Hu-*man*!' And then: '*Be*-ing! *Be*-ing! *Be*-ing!' Afterwards, his sudden anger forcing the rugby team to offer her protection.

Avril, during readings, almost off-stage. Too tiny for seats, preferring to stand by the inner door. Glass in hand. Weight on one leg. As though an afterthought of hers to peer back in at us.

In the wake of a poem, the usual few seconds of silence.

Then her refrain: 'Could you read that for us again?'

Her fondness for puns no matter how irrelevant: 'Yes, you see... (hand held up to head) '... I know that when you use the word 'sole', you mean...' (hand half-outstretched) '...the *footsole*, of course, of course...' (hand back to head) '...but I was thinking, you see...' (both hands fully outstretched) '...of the other 'soul'. Do you... am I... is this making sense?'

Her own poems, wry, angular. Tiny, wound-up extensions of herself, knots and twists of her favourite topics: Italy, illness, devotion. Her first collection, though, always in the offing, indefinitely 'postponed', somehow lacking the confidence and the luck to have it published. Yet encouraging everyone to send their manuscripts off. 'You know, you might want to try *Agenda*.' Encouraging you.

In the background, St Hugh's. The shorn-off atmosphere of an ex-women's college. Cosmically slow play of class and repression. Arched Jean Brodie eyebrows. Long skirts. Smirks. Her boyish, cat-squawking short-circuitry of it all too willed to be comfortable. And, farther back, in childhood, a hinted-at unhappiness… making The Shop her refuge too. Her mixture of strength and weakness magnifying every student's strength and weakness. Parent and child in one.

Your later period in Oxford more settled, more secure, the need for The Shop receding. Your book out. Her retirement. The Shop's new location in her own home—only a couple of streets from college, but too far for casual student drop-ins. Your visits, their visits, dwindling all the time. Her health, always shaky, in decline—'I'm dying, but I'm alright'—holding on to all the cards, memories, and photos of her 'little ones'.

She drank.

'Could you read that for us again?'

# Listen, Battlers, It's All a Big Mission

Yes, it was 'Henry! River! Three o'clock!' and 'Village,
Ollie! Village!' There were bulging eyes
across the tumble drier. — 'My blood is
purer than yours!' — From lane-end to lane-end
they left a black stream — 'Hail to the Chief
of the Church Walk Challenge!' — as typewritten notes
swept over the freezer. — 'Please! The kitchen
is for *everyone*!' — And lounging in cloisters
they floated with clouds, — 'I want to teach
computers to sing...' — in lava-lamp slices
they let their eyes swim — 'Yes, I really *am*
a rocket scientist.' — and over the 'untrue'
table they boomed: 'I can do sunflowers better
than Mother Nature!' They sauntered in

before the lecture (with spots of river going
nowhere on their skin) to admit:
'You could feel the middle-class shutters
crashing down...' They memorised everybody's
middle name, they stared along the Broad
with the enhanced peripheral vision of
little brothers. They ploughed into railings. They
sank to the floor. — 'Go on. Take my Queen.
See if I care!' — They sang 'I am a C!' They
sang 'I am a C!' — They bothered little pubs
on Sunday to admonish beef-and-ale pie,
'I don't really want to be a man of the world.'
They thought about marriage — 'It's the way
forward!' — They flung Mario out of his car,
captured three red mushrooms, and began
to strangle Eddie Jordan in the Rose and Crown. —
'Did you think that I was made of Teflon?' —

It was 'Pick a window!' oh yes, and 'Piss
up a rope!' It was 'Chaps and chapesses.'
It was 'Skip the coffee!' and 'Why you mock me?'
and it was halfway through *The Deer Hunter*
when the voices went: 'Is that Robert De Niro?' —
'Isn't this a one-way street?' — 'It is! It is!
That's Robert De Niro!' — 'The only thing he's
good at is pulling...' — 'Isn't everything?' —
'...and he mings at that...' — They sang, 'I am a C-H!'
They sang, 'I am a C-H!' They promised to be done
by summer, autumn, Christmas of next year,
they fled the chip shop for a tactical chunder —
'Listen, battlers, it's all a big mission...' — they
sped to the traffic-light bop in lincoln green —
'Give the nodders to Jazzy!' — they quit
the all-night poker to chase the morning joggers —
'Early risers, up the arse!' — they weaved — 'Go back
to your Sheffield slums!' — they revived — 'Imagine
I have two envelopes...' — they went for a flying

ankle-job. — 'Get the fat bald bastard! Don't let him
get away with it!' — Yes, Henry, they carolled,
'I am a C-H-R-I-S-T-I-A-N...!' Yes, Ollie,
they mused, 'Do they still remember the war
in Vietnam?' For it was 'Henry', yes, it was
'Ollie', oh yes, and it was 'Village' — 'Oh no,
it's not The Real World, no...' — '...and I have
C-H-R-I-S-T in my H-E-A-R-T...' — 'But it is
*a* real world' — 'One envelope contains
twice as much as the other, right? I hand you
an envelope. I say that it contains five pounds.' —
'...and I will L-I-V-E-E-T-E-R-N-A-L-L-Y!' —
'So. Do you want to swap?'

# Longer Darker and Richer

All the shadows that I made across the city
were one shadow.
All the shadows that the city made
were one.
All the shadows of a frisbee
drifting back
as planned, every shadow
of a ladybird
lifting off St Anne's,
all the shadows of a street-wide cloud
blotting out a street
were one shadow.
All the shadows leaping from bridges
to celebrate, all the shadows
twisting Shakespeare to fascinate,
all the shadows of chimney tops,
of double chins, of gargoyles
and of gardening shears. Every
pear-shadow bulging, every hat-shadow
tumbling, the entire
spectrum of don-shadows, van-shadows, pin-shadows
were one shadow.
All the shadows of a doubt,
every shadow of a lie,
the thick shadows of mathematical proof
broken by the shadow of design,
the shadows geometrically sharp and steep,
the shadows that blew away,
every shadow of a briefcase
pursuing the shadow of every train.
All the shadows that we might have been
and all the shadows we became
made one shadow

that was long and dark and rich:
the shadow of Oxford as it wheeled throughout the day—
although longer and darker and richer

was the shadow of the city's name.

# The Cigarettes of Others

Beneath the night-foxes of North Parade,
Michaelmas Sunday in the sudden rain.

Beneath elephant-skin and tortoiseshell,

the last time I saw the first friend I made.
Beneath the below, the above begins

with an overtaking whiteness in the underpass,

that streak of recklessness we never had,
(well, so be it) as we race back in time,

piercing the dark with the cigarettes of others —
those nights we left the spinning yard of ale

for late kebab-van ice cream. Let's steer
again to that village where the next world

is the past, to be lost with the night-cats
of North Parade — beneath the cars parked

with mirrors folded in, beneath the churches

bending in the air like bird-flocks. Let's flick
a matchbox over the depthless glass until it

stands on end, step out beneath a sky
of fallen leaves, a sun of exploding clay.

Put the below above, put the above away.

# Acknowledgements

I would like to thank the editors of the following publications in which some of these poems appeared: *Poetry Review*, *Poetry Ireland Review*, *PN Review*, *The Yellow Nib*, *The Wolf*, *Manchester Review*, *Digital Behemoth*, and *Connotation Press: An Online Artifact*.